American Scenes

AND OTHER POEMS

CHARLES TOMLINSON

American Scenes

AND OTHER POEMS

LONDON
OXFORD UNIVERSITY PRESS
NEW YORK TORONTO

Oxford University Press, Ely House, London W. 1

GLASGOW NEW YORK TORONTO MELBOURNE WELLINGTON
CAPE TOWN SALISBURY IBADAN NAIROBI LUSAKA ADDIS ABABA
BOMBAY CALCUTTA MADRAS KARACHI LAHORE DACCA
KUALA LUMPUR HONG KONG

© *Oxford University Press 1966*

First printed in 1966
Reprinted in 1966

PRINTED IN GREAT BRITAIN
AT THE UNIVERSITY PRESS, OXFORD
BY VIVIAN RIDLER
PRINTER TO THE UNIVERSITY

TO MY PARENTS

CONTENTS

I. NEGOTIATIONS

II. AMERICAN SCENES

III. MEXICAN POEMS

IV. IN CONCLUSION

ACKNOWLEDGEMENTS

ACKNOWLEDGEMENTS are due to the editors of the following anthologies and periodicals in which some of these poems first appeared: *Agenda, The Critical Quarterly, Encounter, Hudson Review, London Magazine, New Statesman, Paris Review, P.E.N. New Poems 1965, Poetry Chicago, The Resuscitator,* and *The Times Literary Supplement.*

I must also express my gratitude to the University of New Mexico whose D. H. Lawrence Fellowship facilitated the writing of several of these poems.

I. NEGOTIATIONS

FACE AND IMAGE

BETWEEN
the image of it
and your face: Between
is the unchartable country,
variable, virgin
terror and territory.

The image—
that most desperate act
of portraiture—
I carry and my mind
marries it willingly,
though the forfeiture's
foreknown already: admit
the reality and you see
the distance from it.

The face—
mouth, eyes and forehead,
substantial things,
advance their frontier
clear against all imaginings:

And yet—
seeing a face, what
do we see?
It is not
the one
incontrovertible you or me.

For, still, we must
in all the trust of seeing
trace
the face in the image, image in the face.

To love
is to see,
to let be
this disparateness
and to live within
the unrestricted boundary between.

Even an uncherished face
forces us
to acknowledge
its distinctness, its continuance thus;
then how should these
lips not compound the theme
and being of all appearances?

THE SNOW FENCES

THEY are fencing the upland against
the drifts this wind, those clouds
would bury it under: brow and bone
know already that levelling zero
as you go, an aching skeleton,
in the breathtaking rareness of winter air.

Walking here, what do you see?
Little more, through wind-teased eyes,
than a black, iron tree
and, there, another, a straggle
of low and broken wall between, grass
sapped of its greenness, day going.

The farms are few: spread
as wide, perhaps, as when
the Saxons who found them, chose
these airy and woodless spaces
and froze here before they fed
the unsuperseded burial ground.

Ahead, the church's dead-white
limewash will dazzle the mind
as, dazed, you enter to escape:
despite the stillness here, the chill
of wash-light scarcely seems
less penetrant than the hill-top wind.

Between the graves, you find
a beheaded pigeon, the blood and grain
trailed from its bitten crop, as alien to all
the day's pallor as the raw
wounds of the earth, turned above
a fresh solitary burial.

A plaque of staining metal
distinguishes this grave among
an anonymity whose stones
the frosts have scaled, thrusting under
as if they grudged the ground
its ill-kept memorials.

The bitter darkness drives you
back valleywards, and again you bend
joint and tendon to encounter
the wind's force and leave behind
the nameless stones, the snow-shrouds
of a waste season: they are fencing
the upland against those years, those clouds.

THE FOX

WHEN I saw the fox, it was kneeling
in snow: there was nothing to confess
that, tipped on its broken forepaws
the thing was dead—save for its stillness.

A drift, confronting me, leaned down
across the hill-top field. The wind
had scarped it into a pennine wholly of snow, and
where did the hill go now?

There was no way round:
I drew booted legs
back out of it, took to my tracks again,
but already a million blown snow-motes were
        flowing and filling them in.

5

Domed at the summit, then tapering,
the drift still mocked
my mind as if the whole
fox-infested hill were the skull of a fox.

Scallops and dips
of pure pile rippled and shone, but what
should I do with such beauty
eyed by that?

It was like clambering between its white temples
as the crosswind tore
at one's knees, and each
missed step was a plunge at the hill's blinding interior.

BONE

I UNEARTHED
what seemed like the jawbone of an ass—
and what a weapon it was
that Samson wielded! For the first time
as I drew the soil-stained
haft of it out, I knew.

It balanced
like a hand-scythe, bladed
weighted and curved for an easy blow
that would transmit
the whole of the arm's force as it rose
dropped and dealt it.

How many
was it he slaughtered thus
in a single bout
with just such a boomerang of teeth
grained, greened and barbarous?

But no. Not until I'd cleaned
the weapon did I see
how candidly fleshless
that jawbone must have shone
out of the desert brightness.

A sill now restores it
into perspective, emblem
for a quarrel of deadmen where it lies,
brilliant obstacle beside its shadow
across the pathway of appearances.

WIND

INSISTENCE being of its nature,
thus a refusal to insist is to meet it
on equal terms. For one is neither
bull to bellow with it, nor barometer
to slide, accommodated, into the mood's trough
once the thing has departed. The woods
shook, as though it were the day
of wrath that furrowed its sentence
in the rippled forms, the bleached
obliquity of the winter grass.
Black branches were staggering
and climbing the air, rattling
on one another like a hailfall:
they clawed and tapped, as if the whole
blind company of the dead
bound in its lime, had risen
to repossess this ground. As if—
but time was in mid-career
streaming through space: the dead
were lying in customary quiet.
Kin to the sole bird abroad
gone tinily over like a flung stone,
one hung there against the wind,
blown to a judgment, yes, brought
to bear fronting the airs' commotion.
The noise above, and the rooted silence
under it, poised one in place,
and time said: 'I rescind
the centuries with now,' and space
banishing one from there to here:
'You are not God. You are not the wind.'

THE DOOR

Too little
has been said
of the door, its one
face turned to the night's
downpour and its other
to the shift and glisten of firelight.

Air, clasped
by this cover
into the room's book,
is filled by the turning
pages of dark and fire
as the wind shoulders the panels, or unsteadies that burning.

Not only
the storm's
breakwater, but the sudden
frontier to our concurrences, appearances,
and as full of the offer of space
as the view through a cromlech is.

For doors
are both frame and monument
to our spent time,
and too little
has been said
of our coming through and leaving by them.

ONE WORLD

One world you say
eyeing the way the air
inherits it. The year
is dying and the grass
dead that the sunlight burnishes
and breeds distinctions in. Against
its withered grain the shadow
pits and threads it, and your one
lies tracked and tussocked, disparate,
abiding in, yet not obedient
to your whim. Your quiet ministers
to windless air, but the ear
pricks at an under-stir
as the leaves clench tighter
in their shrivellings. The breath of circumstance
is warm, a greeting in their going
and under each death, a birth.

THE WEATHERCOCKS

BITTEN and burned into mirrors of thin gold,
the weathercocks, blind from the weather,
have their days of seeing as they
grind round on their swivels.

A consciousness of pure metal
begins to melt when (say)
that light 'which never was'
begins to be

And catches the snow's accents
in each dip and lap, and the wide
stains on the thawed ploughland are like continents
across a rumpled map.

Their gold eyes hurt
at the corduroy lines come clear whose grain
feels its way over the shapes of the rises
joining one brown accord of stain and stain.

And the patterning stretches, flown
out on a wing of afternoon cloud that the sun
is changing to sea-wet sandflats,
hummocked in tiny dunes like the snow half-gone—

As if the sole wish of the light
were to harrow with mind matter, to shock
wide the glance of the tree-knots and the stone-eyes
the sun is bathing, to waken the weathercocks.

THE HILL

Do not call to her there,
but let her go
bearing our question
in her climb: what does she
confer on the hill, the hill on her?

It shrinks
the personal act and yet
it magnifies
by its barrenly fertile sweep
her very fact.

She
alone, unnamed (as it were),
in making her thought's theme
that thrust and rise,
is bestowing a name:

She inclines
against the current of its resistance,
(as simple as walking, this)
and her bridge-leaner's stance
subdues it with (almost) a willessness.

Nature is hard. Neither the mind
nor the touch can penetrate
to a defenceless part;
but, held on the giant palm, one may negotiate
and she, rising athwart it, is showing the art.

So, do not call to her there:
let her go on,
whom the early sun
is climbing up with to the hill's crown—
she, who did not make it, yet can make
the sun go down by coming down.

A GIVEN GRACE

Two cups,
a given grace,
afloat and white
on the mahogany pool
of table. They unclench
the mind, filling it
with themselves.
Though common ware,
these rare reflections,
coolness of brown
so strengthens and refines
the burning of their white,
you would not wish
them other than they are—
you, who are challenged
and replenished by
those empty vessels.

FRUIT, FOR SCULPTURE

A HALF pear, cool
finial finger
of lute-shaped
abiding fruit.

To eat it?
Who would stir
the white, lit
fallen citadel of its flesh

Without (first)
the thirst of mind and hand
had slaked on
the perfect collusion
of light, knife and tone?

Only
in Eden, does there
ripen a pear of stone.

SAVING THE APPEARANCES

THE horse is white. Or it
appears to be under this
November light that could
well be October. It goes
as nimbly as a spider does
but it is gainly: the great
field makes it small
so that it seems
to crawl out of the distance
and to grow not larger
but less slow. Stains
on its sides show where
the mud is and the power
now overmasters the fragility
of its earlier bearing. Tall
it shudders over one and bends
a full neck, cropping
the foreground, blotting
the whole space back
behind those pounding feet.
Mounted, one feels the sky
as much the measure of the event
as the field had been, and all
the divisions of the indivisible
unite again, or seem
to do as when the approaching
horse was white, on this
November unsombre day
where what appears, is.

THROUGH CLOSED EYES

LIGHT burns through blood:
a shuttering of shadow brings
the cloud behind the retina, and through
a double darkness, climbs
by the ascent the image is descending
a faceless possible, a form
seeking its sustenance in space.

IN WINTER WOODS

1. *Snow Sequence*

A just-on-the-brink-of-snow feel,
a not-quite-real
access of late daylight. I tread
the puddles' hardness: rents
spread into yard-long splinters—
galactic explosions, outwards
from the stark, amoebic
shapes that air has pocketed
under ice. Even the sky
marbles to accord with grass
and frosted tree: the angles
of the world would be all knives, had not
the mist come up
to turn their edges,
just as the sun began
to slide from this precipice, this pause:
first flakes simultaneously
undid the stillness, scattering
across the disk
that hung, then dropped,
a collapsing bale-fire-red
behind the rimed, now snow-spanned
depth of a disappearing woodland.

2. *The Meeting*

Two stand
admiring morning.
A third, unseen as yet
approaches across upland
that a hill and a hill's wood
hide. The two
halving a mutual good,
both watch a sun
entering sideways
the slope of birches
a valley divides them from.
A gauzy steam
smokes from the slope: this
and the light's obliquity
puzzle their glance; they see
thin tree stems:
the knuckled twiggery above
(relieved on sky)
rises more solid
than the thread-fine boles
supporting it—boles that the eye
through its shuttered pane
construes as parallel
scratchings, gold runnels
of paint-drip on the sombre
plane of deeper dark
where the wood evades
the morning. 'But who is this?'
As the third climbs in
down the slope, and the sunlight
clambers with him, on face
and form, 'Who is this?'
they say, who should have asked
'What does he see?' and turned
to answer: a high, bare
unlit hill behind
two faceless visitants
sharing a giant shadow
the night has left: two
at an unseen door
stilled by their question,

whom movement suddenly
humanizes as they
begin descending
through a common day
on to the valley floor.

3. *Nocturnal*

Shade confounds shadow now. Blue
is the last tone left
in a wide view
dimming in shrinking vista.
Birds, crossing it,
lose themselves rapidly
behind coverts where all the lines
are tangled, the tangles
hung with a halo of cold dew.
The sun smearily edges
out of the west, and a moon
risen already, will soon
take up to tell in its own style
this tale of confusions:
that light which seemed
to have drawn out after it
all space, melting in horizontals,
must yield now
to a new, tall beam,
a single, judicious eye: it will have
roof behind roof once more, and these
shadows of buildings
must be blocked-in
and ruled with black, and shadows
of black iron must flow
beneath the wrought-iron trees.

4. *Focus*

Morning has gone
before the day begins,
leaving an aftermath

of mist, a battleground
burnt-out, still smoking: mist
on the woodslopes like a blue
dank bloom that hazes
a long-browned photograph:
under that monotone
sleep ochres, reds,
and (to the eye
that sees) a burning
of verdure at the vapour's edge
seems to ignite
those half-reluctant tones—
then, having kindled
fails them. Green
in that grey contagion
leads the eye
homewards, to where a black
cut block of fallen beech
turns, in the weathers,
to a muddy anvil:
there, the whole, gigantic
aperture of the day
shuts down to a single
brilliant orifice: a green
glares up through this
out of a dark of whiteness
from the log—a moss
that runs with the grain-mark, whirled
like a river
over a scape of rapids
into a pool of mingling
vortices. And the mind
that swimmer, unabashed
by season, encounters
on entering, places
as intimate as a fire's
interior palaces: an Eden
on whose emerald tinder,
unblinded and unbounded
from the dominance of white,
the heart's eye enkindles.

II. AMERICAN SCENES

for Justine and Juergen,
Rita and Franklin

THE CAVERN

OBLITERATE
mythology as you unwind
this mountain-interior
into the negative-dark mind,
as there
the gypsum's snow
the limestone stair
and boneyard landscape grow
into the identity of flesh.

Pulse of the water-drop,
veils and scales, fins
and flakes of the forming
leprous rock,
how should these
inhuman, turn
human with such chill affinities?

Hard to the hand,
these mosses not of moss,
but nostrils, pits
of eyes, faces
in flight and prints
of feet where no feet ever were,
elude the mind's
hollow that would contain
this canyon within a mountain.

Not far
enough from the familiar,
press
in under a deeper dark until
the curtained sex
the arch, the streaming buttress
have become
the self's unnameable and shaping home

ARIZONA DESERT

Eye
drinks the dry orange ground,
the cowskull
bound to it by shade:
sun-warped, the layers
of flaked and broken bone
unclench into petals,
into eyelids of limestone:

Blind glitter
that sees
spaces and steppes expand
of the purgatories possible
to us and
impossible.

Upended trees
in the Hopi's desert orchard
betoken
unceasing unspoken war,
return
the levelling light,
imageless arbiter.

A dead snake
pulsates again
as, hidden, the beetles' hunger
mines through the tunnel of its drying skin.

Here, to be,
is to sound
patience deviously
and follow
like the irregular corn
the water underground.

Villages
from mud and stone
parch back
to the dust they humanize
and mean

marriage, a loving lease
on sand, sun, rock and
Hopi
means peace.

A DEATH IN THE DESERT

in memory of Homer Vance

THERE are no crosses
on the Hopi graves. They lie
shallowly
under a scattering
of small boulders. The sky
over the desert
with its sand-grain stars
and the immense equality
between
desert and desert sky,
seem
a scope and ritual
enough to stem
death and to be its equal.

'Homer
is the name,' said
the old Hopi doll-maker.
I met him in summer. He was dead
when I came back that autumn.

He had sat
like an Olympian
in his cool room
on the rock-roof of the world,
beyond the snatch
of circumstance
and was to die
beating a burro out of his corn-patch.

'That',
said his neighbour
'was a week ago'. And the week
that lay
uncrossably between us
stretched into sand,
into the spread
of the endless
waterless sea-bed beneath
whose space outpacing sight
receded as speechless and as wide as death.

ON THE MOUNTAIN

NOBODY there:
no body,
thin aromatic air
pricking the wide nostrils
that inhale the dark.

Blank brow freezing
where the blaze of snow
carries beyond the summit
up over a satin cloud meadow
to confront the moon.

Nobody sees
the snow-free tree-line,
the aspens weightlessly shivering
and the surrounding pine
that, hardly
lifting their heavy
pagodas of leaves,
yet make a continuous
sound as of sea-wash
around the mountain lake.

And nobody climbs
the dry collapsing ledges
down to the place
to stand
in solitary, sharpened reflection
save for that swaying moon-face.

Somebody
finding nobody there
found gold also:
gold gone, he
(stark in his own redundancy)
must needs go too
and here, sun-warped
and riddled by moon, decays
his house which nobody occupies.

LAS TRAMPAS U.S.A.

for Robert and Priscilla Bunker

    I GO through hollyhocks
in a dry garden, up
to the house,
knock, then ask
in English for the key
to Las Trampas church.
The old woman
says in Spanish: I
do not speak English
so I say: Where
is the church key
in Spanish.
—You see those
three men working: you
ask them. She
goes in, I
go on
preparing to ask
them in Spanish:

Hi, they say
in American. Hello
I say and ask
them in English
where is the key
to the church and they
say: He has it
gesturing to a fourth
man working
hoeing a corn-field
nearby, and to him
(in Spanish): Where is
the church key? And he:
I have it.—O.K.
they say in
Spanish-American:
You bring it (and
to me in English)
He'll bring it. You
wait for him
by the church door.
Thank you, I say and they
reply in American
You're welcome. I go
once more and
await in shadow
the key: he
who brings it is not
he of the hoe, but
one of the three
men working, who
with a Castilian grace
ushers me in
to this place
of coolness out
of the August sun.

A PIANO, so long untuned
it sounded like a guitar
was playing *Für Elise*:
the church was locked: graves
on which the only flowers
were the wild ones
except for the everlasting
plastic wreaths and roses,
the bleached dust making
them gaudier than they were
and they were gaudy:

SILVIANO
we loved him
LUCERO

and equal eloquence in
the quotation, twisted and
cut across two pages
in the statuary book:

THY	LIFE
WILL	BE
DO	NE

OLD MAN AT VALDEZ

No books, no songs
belong in the eighty-
year old memory:
he knows where
the Indian graves are
in the woods, recalls
the day the Apaches
crept into Valdez
carrying away
a boy who
forty years later
came back
lacking one arm and said:
'I could hear you all
searching, but I
dursn't cry out
for fear they'd . . .'
The Indians
had trained their prize
to be a one-armed thief.
'And we never did', the old man says,
'see a thief like him
in Valdez.'

New Mexico

MR. BRODSKY

I HAD heard
before, of an
American who would have preferred
to be an Indian;
but not
until Mr. Brodsky, of one
whose professed and long
pondered-on passion
was to become a Scot,
who even sent for haggis and oatcakes
across continent.
Having read him
in Cambridge English
a verse or two
from MacDiarmid,
I was invited
to repeat the reading
before a Burns Night Gathering
where the Balmoral Pipers
of Albuquerque would
play in the haggis
out of its New York tin.
Of course, I said
No. No. I could *not* go
and then
half-regretted I had not been.
But to console
and cure the wish, came
Mr. Brodsky, bringing
his pipes and played
until the immense, distended
bladder of leather seemed
it could barely contain its water—
tears (idle
tears) for the bridal of Annie Laurie
and Morton J. Brodsky.
A bagpipe in a dwelling is
a resonant instrument
and there he stood
lost in the gorse

the heather or whatever
six thousand
miles and more
from the infection's source,
in our neo-New Mexican parlour
where I had heard
before of an
American who would have preferred
to be merely an Indian.

CHIEF STANDING WATER

or my night on the reservation

CHIEF Standing Water
explained it

all to me—
the way he

left the reservation
(he was the only

Indian I ever
knew who

favoured explanation
explanation)

then his
conversion

(*Jesus Saves
Courtesy pays*—

the house
was full of texts)

and his
reversion to

'the ways of my people'
though he had

never (as he said)
forfeited

what civilization
taught him—

the house
was full of books

books like *The Book
of Mormon*

a brochure
on the Coronation

a copy of Blavatsky
(left by a former guest)

—her *Secret Doctrine*:
had he

read it? Oh he
had read

it. I like
my reading

heavy
he said:

he played
his drum

to a song
one hundred thousand

years old—
it told

the way his people
had come

from Yucatan
it predicted

the white-man:
you heard

words
like

Don't know
O.K.

embedded in
the archaic line

quite dis-
tinctly

and listen
he said

there's *Haircut*
and he sang it

again and look
my hair

is cut:
how's that now

for one hundred thousand
years ago

the archaeologists
don't-know-

nothin: and
in farewell:

this is not
he said

a motel but
Mrs. Water and me

we
have our

plans for one
and the next

32

time that
you come

maybe ...
I paid

the bill
and considering

the texts
they lived by

he and
Mrs. Water

it was a
trifle high

(*Jesus pays
Courtesy saves*)

and that was my
night

on the
reservation.

NERVY with neons, the main drag
was all there was. A placeless place.
A faint flavour of Mexico in the tacos
tasting of gasoline. Trucks refuelled
before taking off through space. Someone lived
in the houses with their houseyards wired
like tiny Belsens. The Götterdämmerung
would be like this. No funeral pyres, no choirs
of lost trombones. An Untergang
without a clang, without
a glimmer of gone glory
however dimmed. At the motel desk
was a photograph of Roy Rogers
signed. It was here
he made a stay. He did not
ride away on Trigger
through the high night, the tilted
Pleiades overhead, the polestar low, no
going off until
the eyes of beer-cans
had ceased to glint at him
and the desert darknesses
had quenched the neons. He was spent.
He was content. Down he lay.
The passing trucks patrolled his sleep,
the shifted gears contrived
a muffled fugue against the fading of his day
and his dustless, undishonoured stetson rode
beside the bed,
glowed in the pulsating, never-final twilight
there, at that execrable conjunction
of gasoline and desert air.

ARIZONA HIGHWAY

To become the face of space,
snatching a flowing mask
of emptiness
from where the parallels meet.

One is no more
than invaded transparency, until
on falling asleep, one can feel
them travelling through one still.

The windshield drinks
the telegraphed desert miles,
the tarmac river: tyranny,
glass identity,
devouring and dusty eye,
pure duration, all
transition, transformation.

We have driven into day,
get down to eat:
in a disappearing shadow
under our feet, the dry
pale Sienese reds and oranges
are distinct crystals
that sleep cannot snatch away.

But sleep
expands through senses
that distance has rifled.

When I wake,
hands and head
are in sand, ants are shifting,
inspecting the remains of breakfast,
and on the lips and tongue
burns the fine-ground glass of the sand grains.

TWO VIEWS OF TWO GHOST TOWNS

I

WHY speak of memory and death
on ghost ground? Absences
relieve, release. Speak
of the life that uselessness
has unconstrained. Rusting
to its rails, the vast obese
company engine that will draw
no more, will draw no more:
Keep Off
the warning says, and all
the mob of objects, freed
under the brightly hard
displacement of the desert light
repeat it: the unaxled wheels,
doorless doors and windowless
regard of space. Clear
of the weight of human
meanings, human need,
gradually
houses splinter to the ground
in white and red, two
rotting parallels beneath
the sombre slag-mound.

II

How dry the ghosts
of dryness are. The air
here, tastes of sparseness
and the graveyard stones
are undecorated. To the left
the sea and, right, the shadows
hump and slide, climbing
the mountainside as clouds go over.
The town has moved away,
leaving a bitten hill

where the minehead's visible. Brambles
detain the foot. Ketchum,
Clay, Shoemake, Jebez O'Haskill
and Judge H. Vennigerholz
all (save for the judge's
modest obelisk) marked
by a metal cross; and there are four
crosses of wood, three
wooden stakes (unnamed)
that the sun, the frost, the sea-
wind shred alternately
in sapless scars. How dry
the ghosts of dryness are.

UTE MOUNTAIN

'WHEN I am gone'
the old chief said
'if you need me, call me',
and down he lay, became stone.

They were giants then
(as you may see),
and we
are not the shadows of such men.

The long splayed Indian hair
spread ravelling out
behind the rocky head
in groins, ravines;

petered across the desert plain
through Colorado,
transmitting force
in a single undulant unbroken line

from toe to hair-tip: there
profiled, inclined away from one
are features, foreshortened, and the high
blade of the cheekbone.

Reading it so, the eye
can take the entire great
straddle of mountain-mass,
passing down elbows, knees and feet.

'If you need me, call me.'
His singularity dominates the plain
as we call to our aid his image:
thus men make a mountain.

IN CONNECTICUT

WHITE, these villages. White
their churches without altars. The first snow
falls through a grey-white sky
and birch-twig whiteness turns
whiter against the grey. White
the row of pillars (each
of them is a single tree), the walls
sculptureless. 'This church was gathered
in 1741. In 1742
by act of the General Assembly of Connecticut
this territory was incorporated
and was named Judea.'
The sun passes, the elms
enter as lace shadows, then
go out again. White . . .
'Our minister is fine. He's a minister
in church, and a man outside.'—delivered
with the same shadowless conviction
as her invitation, when
lowering, leaning
out of the window she was cleaning
she had said: 'Our doors
are always open.'

MAINE WINTER

RAVENOUS the flock
who with an artist's
tact, dispose
their crow-blue-black
over the spread of snow—

Trackless, save where
by stalled degrees
a fox flaringly goes
with more of the hunter's caution than
of the hunter's ease.

The flock
have sighted him, are his match
and more, with their artist's eye
and a score of beaks against
a fox, paws clogged, and a single pair of jaws.

And they mass to the red-on-white
conclusion, sweep
down between
a foreground all snow-scene and a distance
all cliff-tearing seascape.

LETTERS FROM AMHERST

for Edith Perry Stamm

LETTERS from Amherst came. They were written
In so peculiar a hand, it seemed
The writer might have learned the script by studying
The famous fossil bird-tracks
In the museum of that college town. Of punctuation
There was little, except for dashes: 'My companion
Is a dog,' they said, 'They are better
Than beings, because they know but do not tell.'

And in the same, bird-like script: 'You think
My gait "spasmodic". I am in danger, sir.
You think me uncontrolled. I have no tribunal.'
Of people: 'They talk of hallowed things aloud
And embarrass my dog. I let them hear
A noiseless noise in the orchard. I work
In my prison where I make
Guests for myself.' The first of these
Letters was unsigned, but sheltered
Within the larger package was a second,
A smaller, containing what the letter lacked—
A signature, written upon a card in pencil,
As if the writer wished
To recede from view as far as possible
In the upstairs room
In the square cool mansion where she wrote
Letters from Amherst . . .

IN LONGFELLOW'S LIBRARY

SAPPHO
and the Venus de Milo
gaze out past
the scintillations from
the central
candelabrum
to where
(on an upper shelf)
plaster Goethe
in a laurel
crown, looks
down divided
from a group
dancing a
tarantella, by
the turquoise butterfly
that Agassiz
brought back

dead: below
these, the busts of
Homer, Aeschylus
and Sophocles still
pedestalled where
they ambushed Hiawatha.

ON ELEVENTH STREET

A MOSAICIST of minute
attentions composed it,
arranged the gravel
walks, where there is not
room for any, and the neat
hedges of privet: the complete
Second Cemetery
of the Spanish and Portuguese
Synagogue, Shearith
Israel, in the City of
New York
eighteen-five to
twenty-nine, could be
cut out, and carried
away by three
men, one at each
corner: a tight
triangle between two
building ends, the third
side a wall, white-washed
topped by a railing, and a gate
in it on to the street.

A GARLAND FOR THOMAS EAKINS

I

HE lived
from his second year
at seventeen twentynine
Mount Vernon Street
Philadelphia
Pennsylvania where
he painted his
father and his sisters
and he died
in Pennsylvania in
Philadelphia at
seventeen twentynine
Mount Vernon Street.

II

Anatomy, perspective
and reflection: a boat
in three inclinations:
to the wind, to the waves
and to the picture-frame.
Those are the problems. What
does a body propose
that a boat does not?

III

Posing the model
for 'The Concert Singer' he
stood her
relative to a grid
placed vertically
behind her. There was a spot
before her
on the wall that
she must look at.

To her dress
by the intersections
of the grid he tied
coloured ribbons, thus
projecting her
like an architect's elevation
on a plane
that was vertical, the canvas
at a right angle
to the eye and perpendicular
to the floor.
What does the man
who sees
trust to
if not the eye? He trusts
to knowledge
to right appearances.

IV

—And what do you think of
that, Mr. Eakins? (A Whistler)
—I think that that
is a very cowardly way to paint.

V

A fat woman
by Reubens
is not a fat
woman but a fiction.

VI

The Eakins portrait
(said Whitman)
sets me down
in correct style
without feathers.
And when they
said to him:

Has Mr. Eakins no
social gifts? he said
to them: What are
'social gifts'?—
The parlour puts
quite its own
measure upon social gifts.

VII

The figures of perception
as against
the figures of elocution.
What they wanted
was to be Medici
in Philadelphia
and they survive
as Philadelphians.

VIII

The accord with that
which asked
only to be recorded:
'How beautiful,' he said,
'an old lady's skin is:
all those wrinkles!'

IX

Only
to be recorded!
and his stare
in the self-portrait
calculates the abyss
in the proposition. He dies
unsatisfied, born
to the stubborn
anguish of
those eyes.

III. MEXICAN POEMS

THE WELL

in a Mexican convent

LEANING on
the parapet stone
Listening down
the long, dark
sheath through which the standing
shaft of water
sends it echoings up
Catching, as it stirs
the steady seethings
that mount and mingle
with surrounding sounds
from the neighbouring
barrack-yard: soldiery
—heirs, no doubt
of the gunnery that gashed
these walls of tattered
frescoes, the bullet-
holes now socketed
deeper by sunlight
and the bright gaps
giving on to the square
and there revealing
strollers in khaki
with their girls Aware
of a well-like
cool throughout
the entire, clear
sunlit ruin,
of the brilliant cupids
above the cistern
that hold up
a baldachin of stone
which is not there
Hearing the tide
of insurrection

47

subside through time
under the still-
painted slogans
*Hemos servido
lealmente
la revolución*

ON A MEXICAN STRAW CHRIST

THIS is not the event. This
Is a man of straw,
The legs straw-thin
The straw-arms shent
And nailed. And yet this dry
Essence of agony must be
Close-grained to the one
They lifted down, when
Consummatum est the event was done.
Below the baroque straw-
Haloed basket-head
And the crown, far more
Like a cap, woven
For a matador than a crown of thorn,
A gap recedes: it makes
A mouth-in pain, the teeth
Within its sideways-slashed
And gritted grin, are
Verticals of straw, and they
Emerge where the mask's
Chin ceases and become
Parallels plunging down, their sum
The body of God. Beneath,
Two feet join in one
Cramped culmination, as if
To say: 'I am the un-
Resurrection and the Death.'

ON THE TLACOLULA BUS

On the Tlacolula bus
'I flew for the Fuehrer'
it says: *Yo volé*
para el Fuehrer signed
Lukenbac in Gothic.
The Fuehrer is dead and Lukenbac
does not drive today:
instead, a Mexican with the brown
face of a Mayan
is in his place and under
a sign *No distraer*
al Operador is
chatting across his shoulder.
Would Lukenbac? And does he
care for this country, or long
for a land of hygiene and Christmas trees
where he would not dare
write up his boast in Gothic?
As we swing
out of the market square
a goat on a string
being led by someone
stops, stands and while
the bus passes by
into history, turns
on the succession of windows
its narrow stare, looking
like Lukenbac in exile.

THE OAXACA BUS

Fiat Voluntas Tua:
over the head of the driver
an altar. No end to it,
the beginning seems to be
Our Lady of Solitude
blessing the crowd
out of a double frame—
gilt and green. Dark
mother by light,
her neighbour, the Guadalupe Virgin
is tucked away under the right-
hand edge as if
to make sure
twice over and (left)
are the legs of a protruding
post-card crucifixion
mothered by both. A cosmos
proliferates outwards
from the mystery, starts
with the minute, twin
sombreros dangling there, each
with embroidered brims
and a blood-red cord
circling the crown of each.
The driving mirror
catches their reflection, carries on
the miraculous composition
with two names—serifs
and flourishes—: *Maria*,
Eugenia: both
inscribed on the glass and
flanked at either end
by rampant rockets
torpedoing moonwards. Again
on either side,
an artificial vine
twines down: it is tied
to rails in the aisle
and, along it, flower—
are they nasturtiums? They are

pink like the bathing dresses
of the cut-out belles
it passes in descending,
their petals are pleated
like the green
of the fringed curtain that borders the windshield:
they are lilies
of the field of Mexico,
plastic godsend,
last flourish
of that first *Fiat* from sister goddesses
and (yes)
the end ...

CONSTITUTION DAY

SUBJECT for Eisenstein
but in reversion:
proletariat
flowing in cinematic streams
all going the wrong way
to pray
to the Dark Virgin of Tepeyac hill.

Ablaze
in his laundered white
an adolescent recites
a poem on the Constitution
and, *Juarez, Madero, C'ardenas*
the names go by
like faces in a fresco
just as Diego
would have painted them. It's all
very bad, but it's a poem.

While the brass band
finger their instruments for another fanfare
—*Juarez, Lopez Mateos*—
penitents come pouring in
to the gold interior and effigy,
deaf to the Day and seeking
the promise of a more than human mercy.

The committee
platformed behind the spouting child
are quite the best-
dressed Mexicans I have seen,
perched there beyond the doom
of the ragged rest—
of God's desolate mother, Eisenstein
dead of a weakened heart
and Stalin rifled from his tomb.

THE BOOTBLACK

W HAT does he think about
down there? His hair is immaculate
and all that I can glimpse
save for a pair of hands
in a mess of turpentine, the back
thin, its twin shoulder-blades
rucking the shirt. What does he see?
Does he see me? Or the penitents
behind him, crossing the plaza
by the Basilica de Guadalupe
and climbing
up into the shrine
taking the steps on shuffled knees?
It's Constitution Day.
Does he care? Does he hear
the processions of bobbing straw sombreros
on sandalled feet
liquid-footed as sheep
feeding the city from the villages?
Ask your questions, and they
reply with smiles you cannot interpret.
He has done
spreading the stain
from naked fingers, has put on
the shine. I say: 'The shoes
are fit for a king.' And he smiles.
Will he be
angry or mirthful when he
inherits the earth?

Mexico City

53

THEORY OF REGRESS

Seven bulls of a Sunday:
corrida for the crowd, carcasses
for the penitentiary. *And you descend*
said Artaud, *to this*
when you began
with human
sacrifice?

IN MICHOACÁN

A poor church
but an obstinate devotion
had filled it
with flowers.

What power drew
those flower-fraught Indians down
by narrow trails
no one knew

Until the earthquake:
after it, the altar
split wide open
like a hell-mouth,

And inside the wreck
there sat
its guardian idol:
squat, smiling, Aztec.

WEEPER IN JALISCO

A CIRCLE of saints, all
hacked, mauled, bound,
bleed in a wooden frieze
under the gloom of the central
dome of gold. They
are in paradise now
and we are not—
baroque feet gone
funnelling up, a blood-
bought, early resurrection
leaving us this
tableau of wounds, the crack
in the universe sealed
behind their flying backs.
We are here, and a woman
sprawls and wails to them
there, the gold screen
glistening, hemming her
under, till her keening
fills the stone ear
of the whole, hollow sanctum
and she is the voice
those wounds cry through
unappeasably bleeding where
her prone back shoulders
the price and weight
of forfeited paradise.

LANDSCAPE

after Octavio Paz

Rock and precipice,
More time than stone, this
Timeless matter.

Through its cicatrices
Falls without moving
Perpetual virgin water.

Immensity reposes here
Rock over rock,
Rocks over air.

The world's manifest
As it is: a sun
Immobile, in the abyss.

Scale of vertigo:
The crags weigh
No more than our shadows.

IV. IN CONCLUSION

IDYLL

Washington Square, San Francisco

A DOOR:
>PER L'UNIVERSO
>>is what it says
above it.
>>You must approach
>>>more nearly
(the statue
>>of Benjamin Franklin watching you)
>>>before you see
La Gloria di Colui
>>*che tutto muove*
>>>PER L'UNIVERSO
—leaning
>>along the lintel—
>>>*penetra e risplende*
across this church
>>for Italian Catholics:
>>>Dante
unscrolling in rhapsody.
>>Cool
>>>the January sun,
that with an intensity
>>the presence of the sea
>>>makes more exact,
chisels the verse with shade
>>and lays
>>>on the grass
a deep and even
>>Californian green,
>>>while a brilliance
throughout the square
>>flatters the meanness of its architecture.
>>>Beyond
there is the flood
>>which skirts this pond
>>>and tugs the ear

towards it: cars
              thick on the gradients of the city
                        shift sun and sound—
a constant ground-bass
              to these provincialisms of the piazza
                        tasting still
of Lerici and Genova.
              Here
                        as there
the old men sit
              in a mingled odour
                        of cheroot and garlic
spitting;
              they share serenity
                        with the cross-legged
Chinese adolescent
              seated between them
                        reading, and whose look
wears the tranquility of consciousness
              forgotten in its object—
                        his book
bears for a title
              SUCCESS
                        in spelling.
How
              does one spell out this
                        che penetra e risplende
from square
              into the hill-side alley-ways
                        around it, where
between tall houses
              children of the Mediterranean
                        and Chinese element
mingle
              their American voices? ...
                        The dictionary
defines idyllium
              as meaning
                        'a piece, descriptive

chiefly of rustic life';
    we
        are in town: here
let it signify
    this poised quiescence, pause
        and possibility in which
the music of the generations
    binds into its skein
        the flowing instant,
while the winter sun
    pursues the shadow
        before a church
whose decoration
    is a quotation from *Paradiso*.

SMALL ACTION POEM

for Robert and Bobbie Creeley

To arrive
        unexpectedly
                from nowhere:
then:
        having done
                what it was
one came for,
        to depart.
                The door
is open now
        that before
                was neither
open
        nor was it there.
                It is like
Chopin
        shaking
                music from the fingers,
making that
        in which
                all is either
technique
        heightened to sorcery
                or nothing but notes.
To arrive
        unexpectedly
                at somewhere
and the final
        chord, the final
                word.